Oh The Things Mommies Do!
What Could Be Better Than Having Two?

Written By Crystal Tompkins
Illustrations By Lindsey Evans

*For Mothers of all varieties, shapes, and sizes-
You are amazing people.*

Mommies make breakfast and tie up your shoes.

They hold your hand on the first day of school.

Mommies play baseball and go to the zoo.

They build blanket castles in the living room.

Oh the things mommies do!
What could be better than having two?

Mommies ice bumps and kiss your boo-boos.

They hold you tight when you're feeling blue.

Mommies make crafts and stick them with glue.

They keep charts to show that you grew.

Oh the things mommies do!
What could be better than having two?

Mommies play hide-and-seek
and cook chicken stew.

They teach you how to follow the rules.

Mommies go hiking and ride in canoes.

They even help you tidy your room.

Oh the things mommies do!
What could be better than having two?

Mommies ride bikes and conquer the flu.

They keep on the fridge
the things that you drew.

Mommies jump on trampolines
and plant gardens too.

They sing your favorite songs with you!

Oh the things mommies do!
What could be better than having two?

Mommies read bedtime stories
and teach you to read too.

They look through telescopes up at the moon.

Mommies give goodnight kisses-
the best ones, it's true!

Most of all they really love you!

Oh the things mommies do!
Aren't you glad that you have two?

The End